KING*f*ISHER

First
Encyclopedia
of
Animals

KING*f*ISHER

Editor Camilla Reid
Designers Steven Laurie, Ana Baillarguet

US editor Aimee Johnson
Proofreader Nikky Twyman

Photography Lyndon Parker, Andy Teare
Prop Organizer Michelle Callan
DTP Operator Primrose Burton

Artwork Archivist Wendy Allison
Assistant Artwork Archivist Steve Robinson
Picture Research Nic Dean

Production Controller Richard Waterhouse
US Production Manager Oonagh Phelan

Cover Design Reg Page

Writers John Farndon, Jon Kirkwood

Consultant Toby Stark
Specialist Consultant Andrew Kemp

**Produced for Kingfisher
by Warrender Grant Publications Ltd**

KINGFISHER

Kingfisher Publications Plc
New Penderel House, 283-288 High Holborn, London WC1V 7HZ
www.kingfisherpub.com

First published by Kingfisher Publications Plc 1998
This edition first published in 2001

2 4 6 8 10 9 7 5 3 1

1TR/0301/TWP/RNB/130ARM

A CIP catalogue record for this book is available from the British Library

ISBN 0 7534 0567 9

Printed in Singapore

Your book

Your *First Encyclopedia of Animals* is the perfect way of finding out all about the exciting world of animals. Packed with fascinating information, interesting activities and brilliant pictures, it can be used for school projects or just for fun.

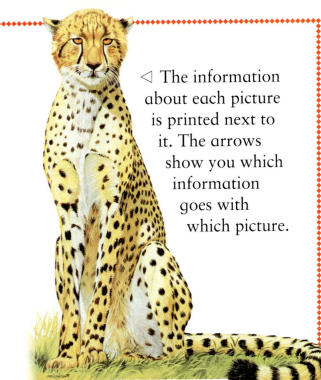

◁ The information about each picture is printed next to it. The arrows show you which information goes with which picture.

◁ Some pictures follow a sequence. Watch out for the numbers to make sure you follow them in the right order.

▽ Step-by-step instructions show you how to do the activities.

Fact box
• These boxes contain extra information, facts and figures.

▷ Labels on some pictures give extra information about the animal. These labels show the points of the horse.

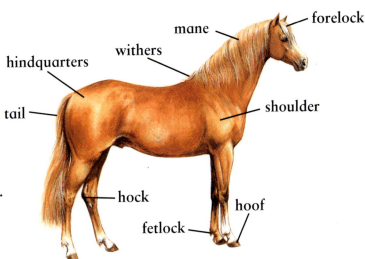

mane

forelock

withers

hindquarters

shoulder

tail

hock

hoof

fetlock

Find out more

If you want to find out more about each topic, look at this box. It will tell you which pages to look at.

Contents

Aardvark

The aardvark is an African mammal that eats termites and ants. Its hearing is so sharp that it can detect these insects moving underground.

◁ The aardvark tears away at termite nests to get at the juicy insects inside. Once the galleries and chambers of the nest are opened up, it quickly licks up the termites.

◁ The word aardvark means 'earth pig' in the Afrikaans language. This name was given to them by Dutch settlers in Africa. Aardvarks are the same size as pigs but they have much larger ears and longer snouts.

◁ Inside the aardvark's huge snout there is a 30-centimetre long, sticky tongue. It is perfect for probing into insect mounds.

◁ Aardvarks live in burrows under the ground. If threatened by a lion, they use their strong claws to dig themselves a deep hole in which to hide.

Find out more
Ant and Termite
Pig

Alligator and Crocodile

Alligators and crocodiles are large reptiles that live in rivers and swamps in tropical areas. They float beneath the surface of the water, with only their eyes and nostrils showing, ready to snap up fish, turtles, and even big mammals in their huge jaws.

△ Crocodiles are cold-blooded creatures that spend much of their lives in the water, keeping cool and hunting. The rest of their time is spent on the riverbank, soaking up the sun's rays. This helps to give them energy.

◁ ▽ The American alligator (left) has a broader and shorter jaw than the crocodile (below). Both alligators and crocodiles have between 60 and 80 teeth in their powerful jaws. They use the teeth to rip their prey to pieces.

Fact box
• Crocodiles have existed for over 200 million years.
• Alligators can grow up to six metres long.
• The largest, crocodile, the saltwater, grows to almost eight metres.

▽ Alligators and crocodiles lay up to 90 eggs in a nest on the riverbank made from mud and leaves. When the young hatch, they call to their mother. She digs them out, picks them up gently in her mouth, and carries them down to the water.

Find out more
Lizard
Reptile
Turtle and Tortoise

Amphibian

Amphibians are animals that live both in the water and on the land. Frogs, toads, newts and caecilians are all amphibians. They are found everywhere except Antarctica, particularly in warm places.

△ Newts have long tails and four short legs, and they look like lizards. However, they do not have scales and their skin is moist.

△ Adult frogs and toads have four legs and no tail. Some frogs inflate their throats to make a loud croak. This helps them to attract a mate.

▷ Caecilians have no legs and resemble worms. They live underground in tropical places. Unlike most amphibians, the female caecilian guards her eggs.

◁ 1 A home-made mini-pond is a great way of attracting frogs and newts to your garden. You will need a washing-up bowl, some sand, pondweed, and a few stones and rocks.

◁ 2 Dig a hole in a corner of your garden and drop the bowl into it. Cover the bottom with the sand and stones, making sure that some of the rocks rise above the surface of the water. Add the pondweed, then fill the bowl with water. Over the next few weeks, watch to see if your pond has any visitors.

Find out more
Fish
Frog and Toad
Habitat
Lizard
Reproduction

Anaconda

The anaconda is one of the largest snakes in the world. It can weigh up to 100 kilograms, which is as much as a large pig. It lives in the jungles of South America, where it hunts in the trees and rivers for food.

▽ The anaconda is called a 'constrictor' because it constricts, or squeezes, its prey to death before swallowing it. Anacondas can catch quite large animals, such as the coypu. A coypu is an animal like a beaver that lives in and near water. The snake will not need to eat for a month after it has eaten a coypu.

△ This anaconda is quite small. The biggest ones are as thick as your waist and five metres long – the same length as a bus.

◁ Snake skin will not stretch like human skin, so the anaconda has to lose its skin as it grows. The old skin splits when it gets too tight, and the snake rubs it off against a branch. Underneath the old skin, there is a shiny new one.

Find out more
Cobra
Rattlesnake

Arctic tern

Arctic terns make the longest of all animal journeys. In autumn, after nesting on the Arctic coastline, these small sea birds fly south to spend a few months fishing on the other side of the world, in the Antarctic Ocean. In spring, they make the long trip north again to breed.

◁ Arctic terns lay two or three eggs in nests on the frozen Arctic ground, or tundra. They defend their eggs and chicks by diving at attacking predators.

△ The Arctic tern's round trip may be more than 36,000 kilometres. But, by being at each pole in summer, it spends nearly all its life in daylight. Chicks hatch in the northern summer, and by autumn they are ready to make the marathon flight south with their parents.

▽ Sooty and fairy terns are found on tropical islands. Unlike Arctic terns, they do not migrate.

sooty tern

fairy tern

Find out more
Bird
Gull
Migration
Puffin

Armadillo

Armadillos are armour-plated mammals related to anteaters and sloths. They are found in regions of North America and all through South America. There are 20 species in all – the largest is the giant armadillo, which is 1.5 metres long.

△ Armadillos live alone, in pairs, or in small groups in burrows. They come out at night to feed. They are easily frightened and bolt for their burrows when threatened.

◁ Armadillos eat many different kinds of plants, insects and small animals. They are fond of ants and termites, which they dig up with their powerful front legs and claws.

▽ When in danger, armadillos roll up into a ball, showing only the hard plates on their head and tail.

Fact box

• Despite their heavy armour, armadillos swim well. To help them float, they swallow air.
• The smallest armadillo is the pink fairy armadillo, which is 16cm long.
• The most common is the nine-banded armadillo.

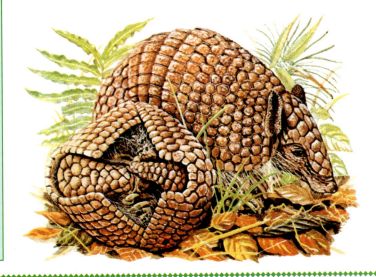

Find out more

Aardvark
Ant and Termite
Hedgehog
Mammal
Porcupine

Baboon

Baboons are large monkeys that live in troops of over 100 in number. They feed on many different foods, from seeds, fruits and grasses to small animals and eggs. They are found in Arabia and in Africa, south of the Sahara.

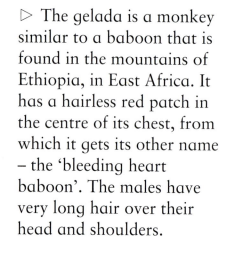

△ Baboons spend much of their time grooming each other. This helps form bonds between babies and mothers, and also between members of the troop. The troop is usually made up of related females, males and one lead male.

▽ Mandrills, from the West African rainforests, are cousins of the baboon. They have bare patches on their large faces. In adult males, these are brightly coloured.

▷ The gelada is a monkey similar to a baboon that is found in the mountains of Ethiopia, in East Africa. It has a hairless red patch in the centre of its chest, from which it gets its other name – the 'bleeding heart baboon'. The males have very long hair over their head and shoulders.

Fact box

• Baboons sometimes weigh 40kg. They can be 1.15m long, and have tails 70cm long.
• Male baboons are twice as big as females.
• Baboons bark like dogs when frightened.

Find out more
Chimpanzee
Gorilla
Monkey
Orang-utan

Baby animal

When they are young, many animals need looking after, just as human babies do. Their parents must keep them safe from harm and find food for them until they are old enough to look after themselves.

△ When danger threatens, the male mouthbreeder fish shelters his young in his mouth. He spits them out as soon as it is safe.

△ The merganser duck sometimes gives its babies a piggyback. This keeps them safe until they are old enough to swim by themselves.

△ A zebra foal must learn to walk straight after it is born so it can follow its mother away from danger. The male zebras will protect the herd by kicking and biting any attackers.

◁ Play the baby penguin game with four or more people. Divide into two teams and stand in rows. The aim is to pass a bean-bag along each row using only your feet. The first team to get the bean-bag along the row wins.

△ Emperor penguins keep their babies warm by carrying them on their feet.

Find out more

Alligator and
Crocodile

Gorilla

Mammal

Penguin

Reptile

Badger

Badgers are powerful creatures, but they are also shy. They are related to skunks and, like them, have black and white markings. In Europe, they live in family groups in woodlands.

▽ Badgers are omnivores, which means that they eat all kinds of food. Their diet includes grasses, fruit and nuts, as well as small animals and eggs. They are good at digging and often catch earthworms.

▽ Badgers are most active in the evening. This is when they come out to feed and to collect straw for bedding.

◁ During the day, badgers stay in burrows called setts. As the group of badgers grows bigger, they dig more underground chambers. Some large setts have been used for hundreds of years.

▷ Unlike the European badger, the American badger lives alone for most of the year in dry, open countryside. It also has a different face pattern.

Find out more
Mole
Raccoon
Skunk

16

Bat

Bats have big ears, furry bodies and wings like leather. They are nocturnal mammals. This means they sleep in caves and attics during the day and fly out to feed at night-time.

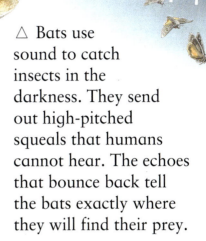

△ Bats use sound to catch insects in the darkness. They send out high-pitched squeals that humans cannot hear. The echoes that bounce back tell the bats exactly where they will find their prey.

▽ Bats are the only mammals that can fly. They are very fast and acrobatic. When they chase after insects, they twist and turn in mid-air.

Fact box
• The 'bumblebee', or hog-nosed, bat may be the world's smallest mammal. It is only two centimetres long.
• The South American vampire bat feeds on the blood of living animals.

▷ Flying foxes, or fruit bats, are large bats that live in tropical Africa and Asia. They mainly eat fruit. Flying foxes are important because they help to spread the pollen and seeds of many plants.

Find out more
Bird
Insect
Mouse

Bear

The bear is the largest meat-eating animal on Earth. There are many kinds of bear and most of them live in northern parts of the world. Their thick fur coats protect them from the cold.

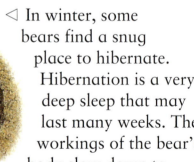
Kodiak bear

brown bear

polar bear

black bear

△ Most bears are large and powerful, with strong claws and a good sense of smell. The Kodiak bear of Alaska is the largest of all. It weighs almost 800 kilograms and, when standing up, can be four metres tall.

◁ In winter, some bears find a snug place to hibernate. Hibernation is a very deep sleep that may last many weeks. The workings of the bear's body slow down to save energy.

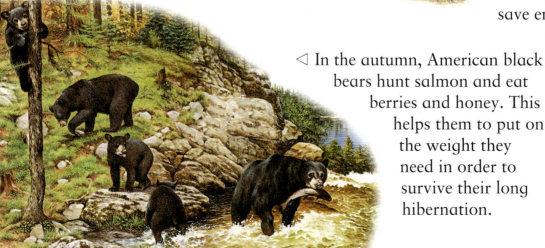

◁ In the autumn, American black bears hunt salmon and eat berries and honey. This helps them to put on the weight they need in order to survive their long hibernation.

Find out more
Mammal
Polar bear
Raccoon

Beaver

Beavers live near rivers in North America and northern Europe. They are great builders and use their massive front teeth to cut down trees. Beavers use these trees to make their homes, which are called lodges.

Fact box

- Beaver dams can be over 500m long and up to 4m high.
- Some beaver dams are 1,000 years old.
- A male and female pair of beavers will stay together for their whole lives.

△ Beavers dam the river with branches to make a pond. In this pond they build a lodge. Beavers use their large, webbed feet and big flat tails to push themselves through the water. If alarmed, they slap their tails on the water to warn other beavers.

◁ Beaver lodges are made of sticks and mud. Beavers seal their lodges with more mud during the winter. The mud freezes hard and helps to keep out predators.

▽ The adults enter the lodge by an underwater entrance and bring food to their young hidden inside. The young beavers will stay with their family for about two years. Then they leave to build their own lodges.

dam

lodge

Find out more

Otter

Platypus

Rabbit and Hare

Rat

Bee and Wasp

Bees and wasps are easy insects to spot because of their black and yellow, or black and white, striped bodies. Wasps and worker bees have a stinging tail. Bees only sting in self-defence and usually die afterwards.

▽ Honeybees are ruled by a queen. They build wax rooms, called cells. **1** The queen lays an egg in each cell. **2** This grows into a larva. **3, 4** The worker bees feed it. **5, 6** Soon it grows into an adult and emerges.

△ Bees collect the sweet juice, or nectar, from flowers and use it to make honey. They keep the honey in cells to feed their growing young.

◁ The bumblebee is larger and more furry than the honeybee. It collects pollen from flowers using its hindlegs. The bee carries the pollen in pollen sacs. Flowers need bees to spread pollen in order to reproduce.

1

2

3

4

5

6

pollen sac

▽ Wasps are different from bees because they feed their young on insects, not honey. They use their sting to kill the insects. Adult wasps eat the sugars found in fruit, and so are attracted by the smell of sweet food or liquids.

Find out more

Fly

Insect

Reproduction

Beetle

There are over a quarter of a million species of beetle in the world. They come in many shapes and sizes, but all have one thing in common – a pair of delicate, folded wings protected by a hard outer casing or shell.

△ Some species of water beetle hunt tadpoles and baby fish. Before diving, the beetles come to the surface to collect air under their wing casings.

◁ Fireflies are not flies, but flying beetles that glow in the dark. They give off light from their abdomen (rear body part) to attract mates. They let out short, regular flashes – each species has its own typical flash pattern. In some of the 1,900 species the female does not fly. She is called a glow-worm.

△ Dung beetles collect a ball of dung and lay an egg in it. When the egg hatches, the new beetle larva eats the dung.

▽ Stag beetles are huge, measuring up to 7.5 centimetres long. The males often fight each other with their large jaws.

Find out more

Ant and Termite
Dragonfly and Damselfly
Fly
Insect

Bird

Birds live all over the world and there are nearly 10,000 species. They are the only animals to have feathers and wings, but not all can fly. All birds lay eggs, and most build nests where they can raise their chicks.

◁ Most birds, like this magpie, have a very light skeleton, strong chest muscles, a tough beak and eyes on the side of the head. Nearly all birds make sounds, called songs, to 'talk' to each other.

▷ Birds have evolved to fit the places where they live and the foods they eat. Birds of prey, like this sparrow-hawk, have strong claws, sharp eyes and hooked beaks to help catch tiny animals hidden in the grass far beneath them.

▽ Birds often have dull feathers to help them hide among their surroundings. But some, like these male birds of paradise, are brightly coloured. This helps them to attract females.

blue bird of paradise

Raggiana bird of paradise

black-billed touraco

△ Many birds live on or near water. The jaçana has large feet and long claws, which help it to walk on floating leaves. Unlike most birds, it is the male jaçana that looks after the eggs, not the female.

rose-ringed parakeet

Find out more

Eagle
Ostrich, Emu and Cassowary
Parrot
Penguin

Buffalo

Buffalo are big, strong, dark-coloured mammals with huge horns. African buffalo live in herds of several hundred – usually near water, as they love to wallow in mud. Water buffalo are found in the wetter areas of Asia. Few are found in the wild now and they are mostly kept as farm animals.

△ African buffalo have very bad tempers, so humans have never managed to tame them.

△ Males are much larger than females. Their horns meet together as a lump on their heads. This helps protect them from any attack. Groups of lions attack females and young, but they will rarely go for a male.

◁ Water buffalo have been domesticated for 3,000 years. They are used to pull carts and ploughs, but they can be kept for their meat, milk and hides. Only a few survive in the wild in Asia, but buffalo released in Australia now run free in the swamps of the Northern Territory.

Find out more
Cow and Bull
Habitat
Lion
Mammal

Butterfly and Moth

These flying insects are found worldwide, especially in warm places. Most butterflies are colourful and fly by day. Moths usually fly at night and are dull in colour.

△ Swallowtail butterflies are so-called because their wings look like the tails of swallows.

1 egg

2 caterpillar

3 pupa

4 adult

△ **1** The female butterfly lays her eggs on a branch and these hatch into caterpillars. **2, 3** The caterpillar eats the leaves and grows fast, until it is ready to spin itself a hard case, called a pupa. **4** Gradually, it starts to change and soon becomes an adult butterfly.

▽ The death's head hawk moth of Africa gets its name from the skull-shaped pattern on its back.

◁ See for yourself how caterpillars turn into butterflies. Collect some caterpillars and put them in a large jar, along with the branches you found them on. Fasten some net across the top with an elastic band. Add fresh leaves every day and watch the changes as they happen. Make sure you let the butterflies go as soon as they can fly.

Find out more
Bee and Wasp
Cricket and Grasshopper
Insect
Reproduction

Camel

Camels live in the world's driest deserts. They have humps of fat on their backs that help them survive for days without food or water.

▽ A camel's feet are big and wide to stop it from sinking into the desert sand.

△ Camels have been used since ancient times to carry people across deserts.

△ A camel has two rows of eyelashes to shield its eyes in a sandstorm. It can also close its nostrils tight.

◁ The Arabian camel, or dromedary, has one hump. The Bactrian camel has two humps. Bactrians live in Central Asia; dromedaries live in North Africa, the Middle East and India.

Find out more
Antelope
Cow and Bull
Giraffe
Llama

Cat (wild)

Apart from the big cats like lions and tigers, most wild members of the cat family are fairly small. Many wild cats are hunted for their boldly patterned coats. Because of this, some are in real danger of extinction and need protection in the wild.

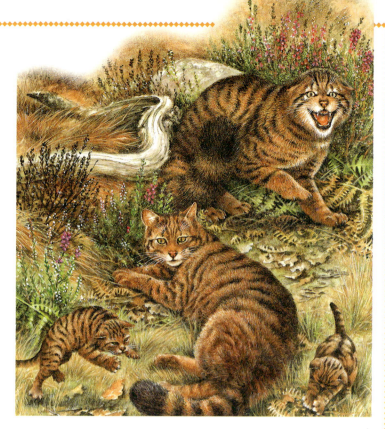

▽ Caracals are cats that live in dry, scrubby areas of India and Africa. They particularly like to eat birds and will often leap up to catch them. The saying 'Putting the cat among the pigeons' comes from the actions of this cat.

△ The European wildcat is found in forests from western Asia, through the continent of Europe, to Scotland. They are nocturnal animals that hunt birds and small mammals for food. The female gives birth to between three and six kittens.

Fact box
• The smallest cat is the rusty-spotted cat, at just 35 centimetres long. It lives in India.
• The fishing cat of India has webbed paws.
• European wildcats can be 40 centimetres at the shoulder and weigh up to ten kilograms.

△ The North American bobcat gets its name from its short (bobbed) tail. It lives in forests and deserts and catches rabbits, mice and squirrels.

Find out more
Cat (domestic)
Leopard
Lion
Tiger

Chameleon

Chameleons are unusual lizards that can change their skin colour. They do this when they are angry or frightened, when the light or temperature levels change, or to hide themselves.

△ There are special cells called melanophores underneath a chameleon's skin. These can change colour to match the chameleon's surroundings, making it more difficult to see.

▽ A chameleon will sit in a tree waiting to catch insects. A strong, curled tail holds it to the branch, while swivelling eyes allow it to see prey in two directions at the same time. Then its long tongue darts out to catch the prey.

Fact box

• There are about 100 species of chameleon.
• Around 50 of these species live on the island of Madagascar.
• Most species of chameleon live in trees, but come down to lay their eggs in the soil.

▷ The Madagascan pygmy chameleon is the smallest species at about 2.5 centimetres long. It lives mainly on leaves on the forest floor. Most chameleons are between 17 and 25 centimetres long, but some can grow up to 60 centimetres. While most chameleons eat insects, the bigger ones also eat birds.

Find out more

Alligator and Crocodile
Camouflage
Lizard
Reptile

Chimpanzee

Chimpanzees, or chimps, are our closest animal relatives, and are some of the most intelligent animals. They live in tropical rainforests and woodlands in Africa. Chimps eat fruits, leaves and seeds, but they also like termites and ants.

△ Chimps sometimes use twigs to prise insects out of their mounds, and will crack nuts open by hitting them with stones.

Fact box

• The tallest male chimps are about 1.6m tall when they stand up – almost as big as a small human adult. Female chimps are shorter.
• Chimps can live to be 60 years old.
• Chimps live in groups. These have between 15 and 80 members.

△ Chimps spend a lot of their time in trees. They use their long arms to swing from branch to branch in search of food. At night, they build nests of leaves to sleep in.

◁ Chimps usually move about on all fours, but they can also walk upright, which leaves their hands free. If attacked, a chimp may defend itself by throwing stones.

Find out more

Baboon
Gorilla
Lemur
Monkey
Orang-utan

32

Cobra

Cobras are poisonous snakes found in Africa, India and Asia. The most deadly cobras are the mambas of Africa. A bite from a mamba will kill unless the victim is given antivenin (an antidote to snake venom) very quickly. Many people die each year from cobra bites.

△ The king cobra is found in areas stretching from southern China to Indonesia. Reaching 5.5 metres in length, it is the world's longest poisonous snake. The female king cobra lays up to 40 eggs.

▷ In India, snake charmers catch common cobras. They play a tune on a pipe and the cobra rises up from the basket to 'dance'.

▽ One of the cobra's main predators is the mongoose. Mongooses move very quickly and can avoid getting bitten. When frightened, the cobra rears up and spreads its hood.

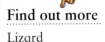

Find out more

Lizard

Rattlesnake

Reptile

Cow and Bull

Female cattle are called cows and the males are called bulls. They are kept on farms all over the world for their meat, called beef, and for their milk. We also use their hides (skin) to make leather shoes and clothes.

Friesian cow

Jersey cow

Hereford bull

Highland cow

△ Female cattle that are reared for their milk are called dairy cows. Twice a day they are brought in from the fields to be milked. Special machines suck the milk from the cow's udder.

△ Although they are not clever animals, cattle are very strong. In many parts of the world, they are used to pull ploughs and carts.

△ There are over 250 breeds of cattle, and each has its own qualities. Friesians give a lot of milk. Jerseys are famous for their rich, creamy milk. Herefords are often used as beef cattle. Highland cattle are tough enough to survive cold winters.

Find out more

Buffalo

Pig

Sheep

Yak

Crab

Crabs are creatures with ten legs and a hard shell. Most live in the sea or along the shore, where they scurry sideways. Their two front legs are frightening pincers, used for feeding and fighting off attackers.

△ Hermit crabs do not have their own shells, but live in the empty shells of sea snails and whelks. As a hermit crab grows, it moves into bigger shells.

▽ Tropical horseshoe crabs are a very ancient species, related to spiders and scorpions. They emerge from the sea in large numbers to lay eggs on the shore.

◁ The legs of some crabs are adapted for swimming. The back legs of this swimmer crab are flattened like tiny paddles.

▷ Fiddler crabs live in muddy mangrove swamps in all regions of the world. One of the male fiddler crab's claws is huge. He waves it to attract females to his burrow.

Find out more
Defence
Scorpion
Shellfish
Spider

Defence

A fast animal can run away from a predator but slower animals need other methods of defence. Thick armour and sharp spines will deter many attackers, as will nasty poisons and bright colours. Other animals simply hide and hope for the best!

△ The porcupine fish inflates its body to make its spines stand out. This will put off most attackers.

◁ The octopus hides in a hole and changes colour to blend into the rock. If spotted, it spreads out its tentacles to make itself look huge and frightening.

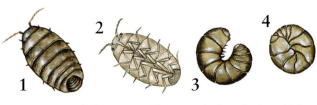

△ The woodlouse defends itself by rolling into a ball so its tough, outer body is all an enemy can see.

▷ A game of hide and seek is very like a hunt between a predator and its prey. The hider will try to make herself as small as possible so that the seeker does not see or hear her.

Fact box

- Animals with a sting or poison are often brightly coloured and have stripes. Predators learn to avoid them.
- Lots of animals use camouflage to hide.

△ A shell acts like a coat of armour for a tortoise. When danger threatens, it pulls its head and legs inside the shell until it is safe to come out.

Find out more

Armadillo
Baby animal
Camouflage
Turtle and
Tortoise

Dog (domestic)

Dogs were domesticated about 12,000 years ago, when cavemen first tamed the Asiatic wolf. Since then, dogs have lived with people wherever they have travelled. They have been bred to help people both in their everyday lives and in their work.

Bernese mountain dog

▷ There are about 400 dog breeds, which are divided into seven groups. These are: sporting dogs, hounds, working dogs, terriers, toy dogs, non-sporting dogs and herding dogs. The Bernese mountain dog is a working dog, the Labrador is a sporting dog and the Yorkshire terrier is a toy dog.

Yorkshire terrier

Labrador

▽ ▷ The collie (below) and the corgi (right) are both herding dogs. Collies help to round up sheep. Corgis once helped to herd cattle. Many collies work on farms, but most corgis are now just pets.

△ Dogs kept as pets should be taught to walk on a lead and house-trained. They must be looked after properly throughout their lives.

Find out more

Cat (domestic)
Dog (wild)
Fox
Hyena
Wolf

Dog (wild)

In many ways wild dogs look and behave like domestic dogs, and they are related. However, wild dogs are usually afraid of humans and cannot be trained. These meat-eaters often live in packs and are found all over the world.

▷ Like most wild dogs, the Cape hunting dogs of East Africa are fierce killers. They have long front teeth for piercing or tearing, and sharp cheek teeth for slicing meat into small chunks. They work in teams to chase down antelope, zebra and wildebeest.

◁ Wild dogs rely on their sense of smell and sharp hearing for hunting. Once they have found their prey's scent, they give chase. Like other dogs, North American coyotes (left) howl to call up the pack for a hunt.

Fact box
- The dhole of India can kill bears and even tigers.
- Golden jackals of southeastern Europe now live mostly on human rubbish.
- The coyote is sometimes called the prairie wolf.

◁ Jackals live in Africa and Asia. They hunt mainly alone at night, and form packs only when there is a chance of sharing a lion's kill.

Find out more
Dog (domestic)
Fox
Wolf

Dolphin

Dolphins are intelligent, graceful sea creatures. They are not fish, but mammals and, like us, they breathe air. They make clicking sounds to help them find their way, catch their prey and communicate.

white-sided dolphin

△ There are over 30 species of dolphin, found in seas all over the world.

Fact box
- A dolphin's top speed is 40 kilometres per hour.
- A dolphin breathes through a blowhole in the top of its head.

spotted dolphin

◁ Dolphins send out sounds in pulses. Then they listen for echoes bounced back from nearby objects to find out what is around them. This way, they can track down fish to eat.

▽ Bottle-nosed dolphins love to play. Like many other dolphin species, their streamlined shape and powerful tails help them speed through the water and they often jump high into the air. They live in big family groups called schools, and like to race alongside boats.

bottle-nosed dolphin

Find out more
Killer whale
Whale

Donkey

Patient and strong, donkeys are used all over the world to carry people and goods. Their small feet and thick coats make them suited to working in dry, rocky places. Because they are quiet animals and gentle with young children, donkeys are often kept as pets.

▽ Donkeys range in colour from almost white to nearly black. They usually have two dark stripes running along their backs and across their shoulders. Unlike horses, only the ends of their tails have long hairs.

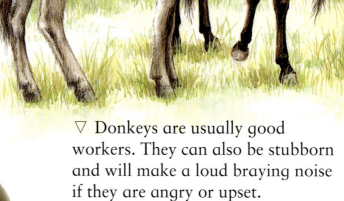

▽ Donkeys are descended from wild asses that were tamed by the ancient Egyptians. Wild asses look very similar to donkeys, with large pointed ears and small hooves. They have thin black stripes on their legs, unlike donkeys.

▽ Donkeys are usually good workers. They can also be stubborn and will make a loud braying noise if they are angry or upset.

Find out more

Horse
Zebra

Dragonfly and Damselfly

Dragonflies are the fastest flying insects, swooping over the streams and ponds where they live at up to 90 kilometres per hour. Damselflies have longer, thinner bodies and are more delicate, with a slow, fluttering flight.

△ Dragonflies and damselflies live near water. The young, called nymphs, hatch from eggs laid on plants. They feed on other water creatures, and after two years the nymphs grow into adults.

▷ The wings of the damselfly are almost transparent. They shimmer as the damselfly searches for small insects to eat.

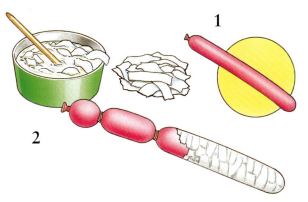

△ 1 To make a model dragonfly start by blowing up a long balloon. 2 Twist and tie the balloon twice to make the three body sections, then cover the balloon with several layers of papier mâché. When this is dry, paint the body.

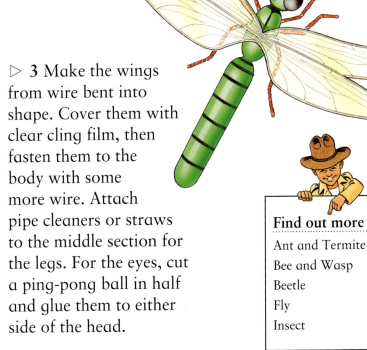

▷ 3 Make the wings from wire bent into shape. Cover them with clear cling film, then fasten them to the body with some more wire. Attach pipe cleaners or straws to the middle section for the legs. For the eyes, cut a ping-pong ball in half and glue them to either side of the head.

Find out more
Ant and Termite
Bee and Wasp
Beetle
Fly
Insect

Duck and Goose

Ducks and geese are water birds. Members of this family live in most parts of the world. They have thick plumage (feathers) to keep them warm, and webbed feet for paddling along in water.

△ Geese are generally bigger than ducks and have longer necks. Geese have big beaks for pulling up and eating grass. Ducks have flatter beaks for sifting food from the water.

◁ Ducks have short legs and they waddle when they walk. Their feet have three front toes in a web and a rear toe that is separate. Almost all duck species live in fresh water. As well as feeding on insects and worms, they eat vegetable matter.

△ Eider ducks breed along icy northern coasts. To keep her eggs warm, the female lines the nest with fluffy feathers (down) plucked from her breast.

▽ Most Canada geese that breed in Canada and Alaska migrate to Mexico and the southern United States in winter. When they fly, they often make a loud honking noise.

△ Male ducks are called drakes. They often have colourful plumage, which is designed to attract females. Female ducks are usually dull brown.

Find out more
Bird
Gull
Migration
Penguin
Swan

Eagle

Strong wings, sharp eyes and powerful talons make eagles great hunters. Their large, hooked bills are used for slicing open and eating – not for killing. They also scavenge if they find dead animals. These big birds of prey are found in regions from the cold Arctic to the warm tropics.

◁ The golden eagle (left) and the white-tailed sea eagle are the most widespread eagle species. They are found in Europe and northern Asia. Like most eagles, they nest on cliffs, raising one or two chicks a year.

△ The North American bald eagle is the national bird of the United States. It is not really bald, but has contrasting white head and brown body feathers. It lives close to lakes, rivers and coasts.

Fact box

• Because they are so strong, eagles have been symbols of war and national power for thousands of years.

• Eagles mate for life and return to use the same nest every year.

▷ Harpy eagles come from the jungles of South America and the South Pacific. They are powerful hunters, eating sloths, macaws and monkeys. The great harpy eagle (right) is the largest eagle.

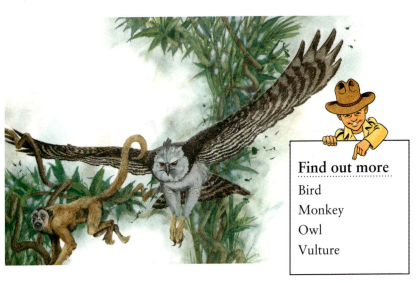

Find out more
Bird
Monkey
Owl
Vulture

Elephant

Elephants are the heaviest land animals. They are also intelligent and have good memories. There are two species: one lives in Africa, the other in India. They use their long trunks almost like an arm, to put food and water in their mouths. Their tusks are made of ivory and males use them for fighting.

△ In India, elephants are trained to do heavy work, such as lifting logs. An elephant driver or keeper is called a mahout.

◁ **1** The African elephant is bigger than its Indian cousin. It has bigger tusks and ears and a hollow forehead. The tusks are really teeth that grow outside the mouth.
◁ **2** The Indian elephant has smaller ears and a rounded forehead. Only the male Indian elephant has tusks.

▽ In Africa, elephants live in small family groups ruled by the oldest females. Males live in all-male herds.

1

2

Fact box

• African elephants grow to four metres, over twice as tall as an adult human.
• They weigh as much as seven tonnes – heavier than six cars.
• Elephants can live to be 70.

Find out more
Giraffe
Hippopotamus
Rhinoceros

Fish

Fish live in saltwater and freshwater all over the world. They come in many different shapes and sizes, but most are covered in scales and have strong fins for swimming.

gills

dorsal fin

tail fin

anal fin

pelvic fin

pectoral fin

◁ Like us, fish need oxygen to live. But instead of breathing air, they absorb the oxygen in water. Water enters the mouth and is swept over the gills. The oxygen passes from the water into tiny blood vessels in the gills.

water out

water in

▽ Fish often swim in groups called shoals. One reason they do this is for protection. Many fish together can confuse a predator, making it hard for it to single out a fish to attack.

▽ 1 A fish's scales all lie in the same direction to help the fish slip through water. You can see how scales work by sticking strips of paper in layers onto a fish outline. (Start from the tail end.)

1

2

△ 2 Now run your hand over the paper scales from head to tail, and then from tail to head. It should feel very different.

Find out more
Jellyfish
Salmon and Trout
Shark

Frog and Toad

Frogs and toads are amphibians so they live both in water and on land. Frogs have moist skins but toads are normally dry. While frogs use their strong back legs for jumping, toads walk. Both animals are good swimmers.

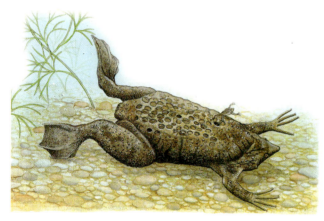

△ The female Surinam toad has special pockets on her back in which her eggs grow. After 80 days, the young toads emerge from the pockets.

△ Many tropical frogs are brightly coloured. This warns other animals that they are poisonous. The poison of the South American poison dart frog (bottom) is so strong that native people put it on the tips of their arrows.

▷ 1 Most frogs and toads lay their eggs, called spawn, in water. 2 After two weeks, tadpoles hatch. 3 Like fish, they breathe through gills, but gradually grow legs. 4 After three months, the gills shrink, the tail gets short and the lungs develop. 5, 6 The tiny frogs are able to leave the water and grow into adults on land.

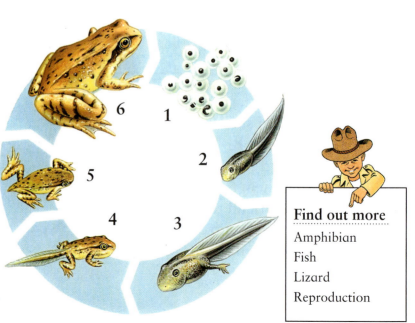

Find out more
Amphibian
Fish
Lizard
Reproduction

Giraffe

Giraffes are the world's tallest animals, measuring up to six metres. Their front legs are so long that they have to spread them wide apart in order to drink at water holes.

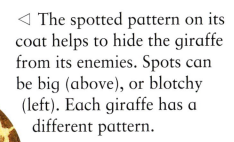

▽ Giraffes live in small family groups on the African plains. About 15 months after mating the female giraffe gives birth to a calf. The calf can get onto its feet and follow its mother only an hour or two after being born.

◁ The spotted pattern on its coat helps to hide the giraffe from its enemies. Spots can be big (above), or blotchy (left). Each giraffe has a different pattern.

△ Giraffes use their height to graze on the leaves at the top of acacia thorn trees. The giraffe tears off the spiky twigs in its tough mouth. It can also curl its long tongue round even higher branches and pull them down to its mouth.

Find out more
Antelope
Camouflage
Zebra

Goat

Goats are hardy and good at climbing, and they can survive in the highest mountains. Wild goats are found across the Northern Hemisphere. Tame goats are kept for their milk, meat and skin.

feral goat

Cretan wild goat

Apennine mountain goat

△ Kashmir and Angora goats are valued for their fine wool. The long, silky coat of the Angora (above) gives mohair or angora wool. Kashmir goats give cashmere wool.

Fact box
• Goats' hooves have hard edges and soft centres. They act like suckers on steep, slippery rocks.
• Goats give off a very strong smell.
• A young goat is a called a kid, a female is a doe or a nanny, and a male is a billy.

△ Goats were first tamed 10,000 years ago, and there are now many breeds. They like to eat grass and plants, but they will eat almost anything and can survive on thorn trees and shrubs. Male goats are often bad-tempered and use their long, curved horns to fight each other for females.

▽ Ibexes are wild goats found in Europe, Africa and Asia. They live on the mountaintops in summer, and move to warmer, lower pastures in winter.

Find out more
Antelope
Cow and Bull
Sheep
Yak

Gorilla

Gorillas are huge and powerful apes. They look fierce, but are actually gentle vegetarians. They are now very rare and are found only in the forests and mountains of Central Africa.

▽ Gorillas live in family groups. These are led by a big male called a silverback, who gets his name from the silver hairs on his back. These hairs grow when a male gorilla is about ten years old. Silverbacks may be as tall as a man and weigh 225 kilograms – about three times as much as a man.

△ Gorillas eat leaves and buds, stalks, berries and sometimes even tree bark. When they have eaten most of the food in one place, they move on to let the plants grow back again.

◁▽ Gorillas learn to walk at about ten months. They feed on their mother's milk for the first two years and spend much of their time playing. They sleep with their mothers until they are three years old, then they make their own nests of leaves and branches.

Find out more
Baboon
Chimpanzee
Monkey
Orang-utan

Habitat

A habitat is the place where an animal lives. It provides the animal with food, water and shelter – everything it needs to survive. There are many different habitats all over the world.

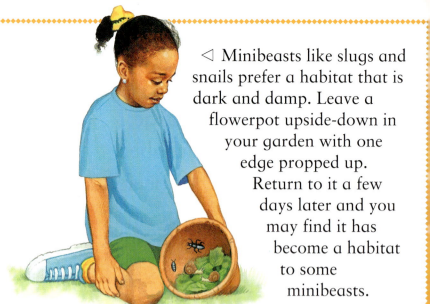

◁ Minibeasts like slugs and snails prefer a habitat that is dark and damp. Leave a flowerpot upside-down in your garden with one edge propped up. Return to it a few days later and you may find it has become a habitat to some minibeasts.

savanna

rainforest

desert

△ Over millions of years, animals have evolved to survive in their own habitats. For example, the camel is able to live in the desert because it can go for days without drinking. If a habitat changes – for example, if the rainfall decreases – each animal must adapt to the new environment. Unlike humans, if an animal is suddenly taken out of its habitat it cannot adapt quickly enough and is unlikely to survive.

Find out more
Camel
Chimpanzee
Giraffe
Slug and snail

Hedgehog

Hedgehogs are mammals found in the woods and hedges of Europe, Asia and Africa. Most have thousands of thick spines covering their backs, which help to protect them from predators. There are also hairy hedgehogs, which live in Asia.

△ Hedgehogs can be friendly, especially if you leave them some dog or cat food. It is best not to touch them, though, as they often carry fleas.

▽ The common hedgehog usually has about four babies. The babies do not get pricked when they drink their mother's milk as she only has spines on her back. Adults go out after dark to hunt for food. They will eat plants, but prefer insects and frogs.

Fact box

• Babies are born blind, with soft spines.
• Hedgehogs spend more than 20 hours a day sleeping. In cold northern regions, they hibernate in winter, curling up under a pile of leaves.
• One hedgehog, the moon rat of Sumatra, can be 40cm long.

△ When a hedgehog senses danger, it curls up into a tight ball with its spines on the outside. This puts off most predators, although many hedgehogs are killed by cars when they curl up on roads. They are able to climb trees and, if they fall, the spines act as a cushion.

Find out more

Fox
Mammal
Mole
Porcupine

Hippopotamus

These huge animals have large barrel-shaped bodies and short legs. The name hippopotamus comes from Greek and means 'river horse'. Although they are not related to horses, they do live near rivers – in Africa.

▷ Hippos spend the day in the water with just their eyes, nose and ears showing. This stops them getting sunburnt. They can stay underwater for up to ten minutes before having to come up for air.

Fact box

• Hippos live in groups of up to 15 in rivers, lakes and ponds across Africa.
• They can grow to 4.6 metres long, stand 1.5 metres at the shoulder and weigh as much as 4.5 tonnes.
• Hippos are related to pigs.

△ Hippos have gigantic mouths with two huge tusks on the bottom jaw. In the breeding season, competing males show off the size of their mouths and may cut each other with their tusks. Hippos leave the water at night and travel to look for the grasses they eat. They have hard lips, which they use to cut the grass.

◁ Baby hippos can weigh 55 kilograms at birth. They can stand within minutes of being born, and must keep close to their mother for protection.

Find out more
Horse
Pig
Rhinoceros

Horse

Long legs, a big heart and large lungs make horses strong and fast – which is why people have used them to ride and to pull carts for 5,000 years. Horses are descended from wild horses that once lived in herds on grassy plains.

dun

dark bay

roan

light bay

palomino

chestnut

piebald

grey

skewbald

black

▷ Horses come in many colours, each with a special name.

◁ Ponies can be kept as family pets. They need a field to live in, and lots of care and attention. They should be exercised regularly and need their hooves trimmed every few weeks.

▽ Grooming keeps a pony's coat glossy and healthy. Be sure never to walk behind a horse or pony – it may kick out in surprise.

▽ Every part, or point, of a horse has a name. Horses are measured in hands. One hand is four inches (about ten centimetres) – the width of a man's hand.

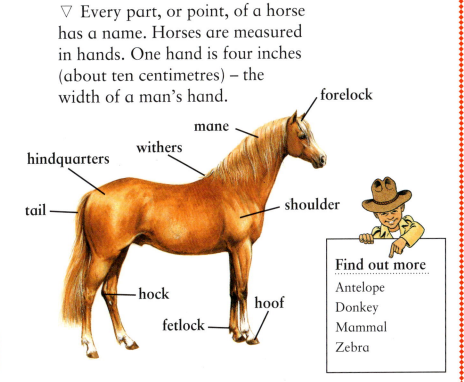

forelock

mane

withers

hindquarters

tail

shoulder

hock

hoof

fetlock

Find out more

Antelope
Donkey
Mammal
Zebra

Hummingbird

When hummingbirds hover, their wings beat so fast that they hum, and this gives them their name. These tiny birds live in warm places in North and South America.

▽ Hummingbirds use their long beaks to reach the nectar deep inside flowers.

◁ Hummingbirds use up so much energy beating their wings that they need to feed often. The nectar they eat is full of sugar, which gives them energy quickly.

△ A hummingbird's wings swivel. This means it can hover near a flower while keeping its head perfectly still. It can also fly backwards.

Fact box

• Ruby-throated hummingbirds fly 800km nonstop across the Gulf of Mexico when migrating.
• Hummingbirds normally lay two eggs, which are the smallest of any bird.
• There are over 300 species of hummingbird.

▷ All hummingbirds are tiny, but the bee hummingbird of Cuba is the world's smallest bird. It is just 5.5 centimetres long – no bigger than a child's thumb.

Find out more
Bird
Kiwi
Ostrich, Emu and Cassowary

Hyena

Hyenas are mammals that live in Africa and Asia. They mainly eat the bones and flesh left by lions after a kill. Their jaws are so strong that they are able to crush and eat bones that even lions cannot manage.

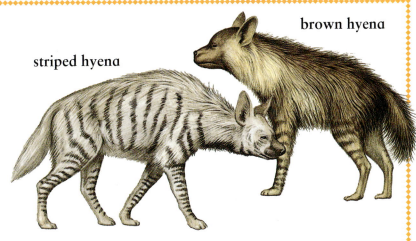

striped hyena

brown hyena

△ Brown and striped hyenas are smaller and less fierce than spotted hyenas. They often prowl around at night, eating the remains of the kills of other animals.

▷ Spotted hyenas are also known as laughing hyenas because of the weird cries they make. The largest and strongest of hyenas, they grow up to two metres long. Spotted hyenas hunt in packs and sometimes they will attack rhinos.

◁ The aardwolf is a close relative of the hyena that lives in southern Africa. It is smaller than a hyena and eats only termites, ants and insects.

Find out more

Dog (wild)

Fox

Lion

Wolf

Insect

There are more insects on Earth than any other group of creatures. There are probably more than a million species and they live in almost every region and habitat in the world.

◁ Insects can carry out complicated tasks and will often build elaborate structures. The potter wasp, for example, builds her nest out of chewed-up wood or mud. She kills caterpillars and brings them back as food for her young.

Fact box
• The smallest insect is the fairy fly, which is just 0.2mm long.
• Mayflies live just a few hours, but some beetles live many years.
• An ant can lift 50 times its own weight.
• The largest cockroaches are about 10cm long.

▷ All insects have six legs, a pair of antennae and a body made of three parts: the head, the thorax and the abdomen. The legs are attached to the thorax. Insects are invertebrates, so instead of having bones the body is encased in a tough shell. Many insects also have two pairs of wings.

antenna

thorax

head

leg

abdomen

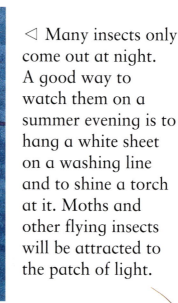

◁ Many insects only come out at night. A good way to watch them on a summer evening is to hang a white sheet on a washing line and to shine a torch at it. Moths and other flying insects will be attracted to the patch of light.

Find out more
Ant and Termite
Bee and Wasp
Beetle
Butterfly and Moth
Fly

Jellyfish

Jellyfish are sea creatures whose soft, wobbly bodies are made almost entirely of water. The smallest jellyfish are just a few centimetres in width, and the largest can measure more than two metres across.

▽ The Australian box jellyfish stuns its prey with its poisonous tentacles. Then it pulls the creature towards its mouth, inside its bell-shaped body.

▽ The Portuguese man-of-war has a bag filled with gas on top of its body. As it floats above the water, the man-of-war trails its tentacles behind it. These tentacles can be up to 50 metres long and are a danger to swimmers as well as fish.

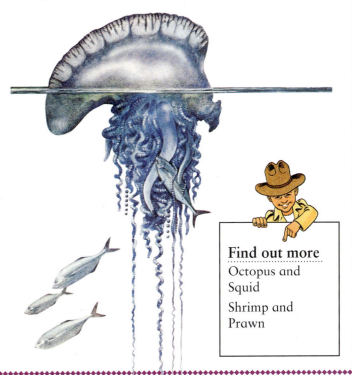

Fact box

• Many humans have been killed by the sting of the Australian box jellyfish.
• Jellyfish are invertebrates. This means that they have no spine (backbone).
• The largest jellyfish measured had tentacles 36.5m long.

△ Some types of jellyfish drift along wherever the ocean currents carry them. But others can propel themselves rapidly by pumping water out from folds in their bodies.

Find out more
Octopus and Squid

Shrimp and Prawn

Kangaroo and Wallaby

Kangaroos and wallabies are marsupials that live in Australia. Marsupial females have pouches on their bellies in which their babies can grow until they are big enough to survive on their own.

▷ A baby kangaroo is called a joey. When it is born, the baby is just two centimetres long. It crawls up to the mother's pouch along a path the mother licks in her fur. Once in the pouch, the joey clings to a teat and stays there until it is large enough to look after itself.

△ There are 56 species of kangaroo and wallaby (the name given to the smaller kangaroos). Most live on the ground, but some live in trees.

▷ Kangaroos are brilliant jumpers. They bound along on their strong back legs, using their long tails for balance. They can jump over ten metres in one leap.

Find out more
Koala, Wombat and Opossum
Mammal
Platypus

Killer whale

Killer whales are the largest members of the dolphin family. They are powerful hunters and can be up to ten metres in length. Killer whales have strong jaws and teeth. They eat fish, dolphins, seals – even other whales.

▽ Killer whales find their way and track their prey by sending out little clicks of sound, then picking up the echo. They live in families called pods. Usually there are ten or so in a pod, but there may be up to 100. Like all whales, killer whales are mammals and give birth to live young.

Fact box
- Killer whales sometimes launch themselves onto a beach to catch seals resting near to the water line.
- One killer whale caught in the Bering Sea had 32 seals in its stomach.
- Killer whales have never killed, or even attacked, humans.

△ Killer whales are fast swimmers, with rounded flippers and strong tails. They can swim at over 55 kilometres per hour, and can jump high out of the water. They live in most of the world's oceans, near the North and South Poles.

Find out more
Dolphin
Mammal
Shark
Whale

Lemur

Lemurs live only on the forested island of Madagascar off the coast of Africa. They are rare because the forests where they live are being destroyed by farmers. Although lemurs look like monkeys with their long tails, they belong to a different family.

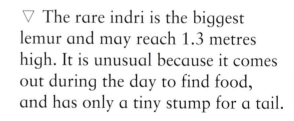

▷ Most lemurs spend their time high up in the trees, but the ring-tailed lemur is often found on the ground. It is the only lemur to have a striped tail, which it uses to signal to other lemurs.

▽ The rare indri is the biggest lemur and may reach 1.3 metres high. It is unusual because it comes out during the day to find food, and has only a tiny stump for a tail.

Fact box

• Lemurs are primates like apes, monkeys and humans.
• Most lemurs like to eat fruit and leaves, but they also eat insects and eggs.
• The smallest lemur is the mouse lemur, at only 15cm long. Most lemurs are around 60cm.

△ Like most lemurs, the aye-aye is active at night, using its big eyes and ears to find food and sense danger. It has an extra-long middle finger on each front paw. It uses this to hook insects and grubs out of holes in trees and to spoon them into its mouth.

Find out more

Chimpanzee
Gorilla
Monkey
Orang-utan

Leopard

Leopards are the most common of all the big cats. They live in forests, deserts, mountains and grasslands, and are found in Africa, India and Asia. They have become rarer in India and Asia because they have been hunted for their striking, spotted coats.

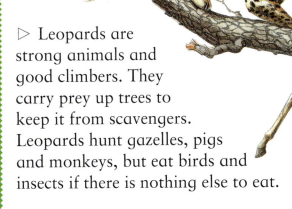

▷ Leopards are strong animals and good climbers. They carry prey up trees to keep it from scavengers. Leopards hunt gazelles, pigs and monkeys, but eat birds and insects if there is nothing else to eat.

△ Leopards usually live alone, with males and females only getting together to mate. Females usually give birth to three cubs. A mother leopard carries her cubs by the scruff of the neck when she needs to move them.

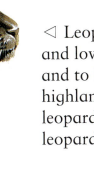

◁ Leopards are great swimmers and love being in water to play and to hunt. In wet areas, like highland and tropical forests, leopards have black fur. These leopards are called panthers.

Find out more
Cheetah
Lion
Mammal
Tiger

Lion

Lions are the largest predators in Africa. These powerful big cats live in groups called prides in bush country or on grassy plains. A pride is made up of several females and their cubs, as well as a few males. Apart from humans, the lion has no enemies and is known as the 'king of the beasts'.

▽ Lions hunt mainly at night and spend the day resting. They prey on many of the large animals of the plains, including antelope, zebra and buffalo. As well as looking after the cubs, the lionesses (female lions) do most of the hunting.

△ The male lion has a large, shaggy mane around its neck. It is his job to defend the territory of his pride and he will warn off intruders with a loud roar. Adult lions have thick tawny-coloured coats, while lion cubs have spots.

Find out more
Cat (wild)
Cheetah
Leopard
Mammal
Tiger

Lizard

Lizards are reptiles. They have scaly skin, long tails and usually live in warm countries. Although they can dart about very quickly, they are cold-blooded and need to lie in the sun to keep warm.

△ The Gila monster is a lizard that lives in the North American deserts. Bright red and black markings warn that it has a poisonous bite.

△ Many lizards turn darker when basking in the sun. This helps their bodies to absorb its heat better.

△ The Australian thorny devil looks frightening, but it is harmless. Its sharp spines save it from being eaten by predators.

◁ The frilled lizard of Australia lifts up its huge neck collar to scare off attackers.

Fact box

• The smallest lizards, the geckos of the Virgin Islands, are 35 millimetres long.
• If some species of lizard are caught by the tail, the tail breaks off. A new one will grow in its place within eight months.

Find out more
Alligator and Crocodile
Chameleon
Reptile

Llama

The llama is found in the high Andes mountains and on the dry plains of South America. Like its relative, the alpaca, it is tame. They are both relatives of the wild guanaco. All three are members of the camel family.

△ Guanacos usually live on mountains over 4,000 metres high, although they are also found on the lower plains. Their blood is rich in red cells, which helps them to breathe the thin mountain air.

△ Today, llamas are used mainly as pack animals, as they were by the ancient Inca people of Peru. Female llamas are used for meat, but the males are too tough to eat.

▷ Alpaca wool is prized by the local South American people. It has a soft feel and provides warmth in the cold climate.

Find out more
Camel
Goat
Mammal
Yak

Mammal

Mammals are a group of animals that includes humans. They are warm-blooded vertebrates and are found all over the world – in the water, on the land and in the air. There are 4,000 species of mammal and they all have certain features in common.

△ A human and a cat are both mammals. They are each covered in hair or fur and they both have a jaw-bone joint which only mammals have.

△ Mammals can be carnivores (meat-eaters), herbivores (plant-eaters) or omnivores (meat- and plant-eaters). This bushbaby is an omnivore that belongs to the primates, a group of mammals that are able to grasp objects with their hands.

▽ All mammals feed their young on milk produced by the female. Apart from animals such as the platypus, all mammals give birth to live young.

▷ Because mammals are warm-blooded, they keep the same body temperature no matter how hot or cold the surroundings. Ask an adult to help you measure your temperature in a warm place and then in a cold place. It should always stay close to 37 degrees centigrade.

Find out more
Baby animal
Platypus
Rabbit and Hare
Reproduction

Mole

Moles are small mammals that spend almost all their lives underground. We know they are around because of the molehills they create when digging their tunnels. They live in Europe, Asia and North America.

△ Big, powerful front paws, a pointed nose and sharp claws mean that moles are excellent diggers. Although they have bad eyesight, they hunt for worms and insects using their good sense of smell and by picking up vibrations with their whiskers.

△ Baby moles are born in a nest, called a fortress, deep below a molehill. They are lucky to be born at all – like all moles, their parents fought furiously when they first met.

◁ When moles dig tunnels they push the earth to the surface, which makes molehills. These are more common in autumn, when young moles look for new areas to live.

Fact box
• Moles surface at night to search for nest material.
• The star-nosed mole has a star of sensitive fleshy tentacles on its nose.
• People used to make clothes from mole fur.

◁ Golden moles are found in dry places in Africa. They live underground and burrow through sand to find food. Like all moles, they have very soft and silky coats.

Find out more
Badger
Mammal
Mouse
Worm

Monkey

Monkeys are clever mammals that can solve problems and hold things in their hands. They live in groups called troops, high in the tropical forests of the Americas, Africa and Asia. Monkeys eat plants, birds' eggs, small animals and insects.

△ A monkey's eyes face forwards, which helps it to see well when hunting. Most monkeys hunt by day.

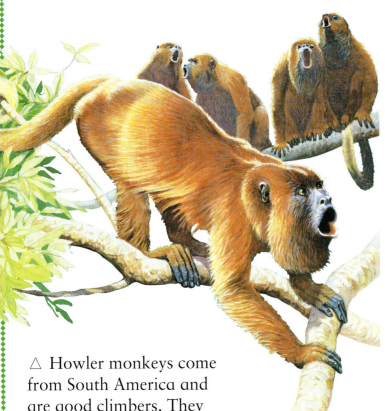

△ Howler monkeys come from South America and are good climbers. They use their tails as an extra 'hand' when swinging through the branches. Howler monkeys live in groups headed by an old male. They get their name from the loud calls the group makes together to warn off other monkeys from their territory.

Fact box

• One difference between monkeys and apes is that monkeys have tails, while apes do not.
• A female monkey usually has one baby or, sometimes, twins.

▷ The capuchin monkey is a small monkey that lives in the Amazon jungle. Because of its intelligence and curious nature, it is often kept as a pet and taught to do tricks.

▽ The proboscis monkey of Borneo gets its name from its big nose. It has a long tail too, but uses it only for balance.

Find out more

Baboon
Chimpanzee
Gorilla
Lemur
Orang-utan

Orang-utan

The word orang-utan means 'man of the forest' in the Malay language, and it is true that this large ape does look a bit like an old, hairy man. Orang-utans live in the rainforests of Southeast Asia.

▷ Baby orang-utans are reared by their mothers and will stay with them until they are around five years old.

△ Orang-utans have become rare partly because their forest habitat has been cut down, but also because some people think baby orang-utans make good pets, and steal them from the wild. Mothers are often killed while defending their babies.

▽ Orang-utans have long, strong arms. They climb slowly through the trees in the morning and evening searching for wild figs – their favourite food. At night they sleep on platforms made of branches.

Find out more
Baboon
Chimpanzee
Gorilla
Monkey

Ostrich, Emu and Cassowary

Not all birds can fly. Although they have small wings, the world's biggest birds – ostriches, cassowaries and emus – can only walk and run.

▽ Emus are the second tallest birds, growing to 1.8 metres. They live on the grasslands of Australia.

▽ Male ostriches are black and white. They are the biggest birds of all – often 2.5 metres tall. Females are slightly smaller and greyish-brown. They can run at 65 kilometres per hour.

△ Ostriches lay up to eight giant eggs in a nest on the ground. The male sits on the eggs at night; the female, during the day.

Fact box

• Ostriches live in Africa.
• Ostrich eggs are the biggest of all bird eggs.

◁ Cassowaries live in the forests of New Guinea and Australia. They are 1.5 metres tall and have featherless heads with a bony helmet on the top. If attacked, they will kick and slash with their clawed feet. Their middle toe is as sharp as a dagger.

Find out more
Bird
Kiwi

Panda

The giant panda is a bear found in just a few high bamboo forests in China. There are probably no more than 1,500 giant pandas left in the wild. About 100 are kept in zoos around the world.

▽ Pandas have one or two cubs at a time. At birth, a cub weighs only 100 grams. At first the mother holds it close to her chest at all times. But it grows quickly and after ten weeks the cub starts to crawl.

△ Giant pandas usually only eat bamboo. To help them grasp the stems, they have an extra pad on their front paws that works like a thumb. Giant pandas have become rare since their forests have been cut down and because they were once hunted for their fur.

▷ Red pandas look very much like raccoons. They live high up in the mountain forests of the Himalayas, from Nepal to China. They feed at night on roots, acorns, bamboo and fruits.

Find out more

Bear
Mammal
Polar bear
Raccoon

Parrot

Parrots live in warm, tropical places around the world. They have strong, hooked beaks for cracking nuts and seeds. Each foot has two pairs of toes, which helps the birds to perch and to grip food.

▷ Macaws are brilliantly coloured parrots from South America. They are large, noisy birds and their piercing screams can often be heard in tropical rainforests.

△ Cockatoos are parrots found in Australia. This sulphur-crested cockatoo has a crest that it can raise and lower. Cockatoos are popular as pets, and often learn to copy human speech.

▷ Lovebirds are brightly coloured small parrots that live in Africa and Madagascar. They get their name from the way they sit together in pairs, resting their heads against each other.

Find out more

Bird
Hummingbird
Peacock
Toucan

Porcupine

Porcupines are covered in spines called quills and this makes them look very much like hedgehogs. However, the two are not related. Porcupines are actually rodents and they have large teeth for gnawing.

△ When a porcupine is threatened, it raises and rattles its quills. If the warning is ignored, the porcupine backs into the attacker and jabs its sharp quills into the animal's flesh.

△ Young porcupines are born with soft quills. As adults, porcupines are about 90 centimetres in length.

▷ Most porcupines have long quills, but the quills of the North American porcupine are short. It lives mainly in forests but also wanders into open countryside. North American porcupines climb trees to feed on leaves, berries and bark, and often strip enough bark from a tree to kill it.

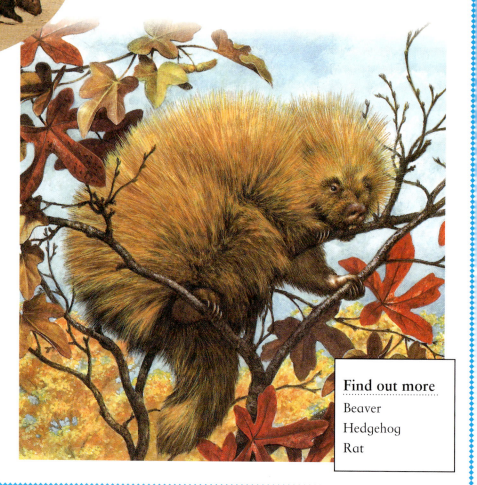

Find out more
Beaver
Hedgehog
Rat

Puffin

Puffins are small sea birds that live in cold northern parts of the Atlantic and Pacific oceans. They have big beaks that become brightly coloured in the summer when they are looking for a mate. In winter the beak is dull yellow.

△ The tufted puffin of the North Pacific is one of only three puffin species in the world. The tuft is made up of long straw-coloured feathers that curve back from behind the bird's eyes.

△ Puffins live in large colonies on clifftops. They nest in long tunnels, which they either dig themselves or take over from rabbits. The females each lay a single egg here.

◁ Puffins feed mainly on sand eels, which they bring back to their nests in their beaks. Although they have a stumpy shape, puffins are fast fliers and swim under-water to catch the eels.

Find out more
Arctic tern
Bird
Duck and Goose
Gull
Penguin

Seahorse

Seahorses are fish that live in warm seas. Because they swim upright and are covered by bony armour, they do not look like fish. However, they are related to the stickleback.

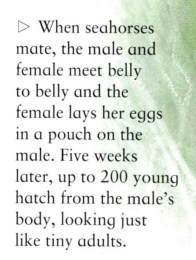

▷ When seahorses mate, the male and female meet belly to belly and the female lays her eggs in a pouch on the male. Five weeks later, up to 200 young hatch from the male's body, looking just like tiny adults.

△Seahorses spend much of their lives anchored by their tails to seaweed. They feed on shrimps and plankton, which they suck into their long mouths.

◁ The sea dragon is a type of seahorse that is found around the Australian coastline. It is 1.5 metres long and camouflaged by leafy-looking growths all over its body.

Find out more
Camouflage
Fish
Reproduction
Shrimp

Seal and Sea lion

Seals and sea lions are good swimmers and divers. They are mammals so they have to come up to breathe, but they can stay underwater for up to 30 minutes. They feed on fish and penguins.

▽ While sea lions can walk on their flippers, seals cannot. Male sea lions have thick fur on their necks that looks like the mane of a lion.

▽ Seals catch their prey underwater, then they come to the surface to eat it.

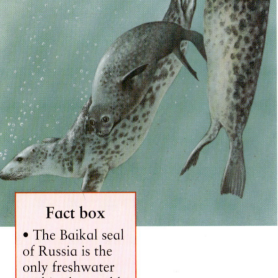

◁ Female seals and sea lions suckle (feed) their babies on milk that is extremely nourishing. The milk is full of fat and helps the babies grow quickly.

▽ Male elephant seals are the largest seals in the world. They get their name from their floppy noses, which look like trunks.

Fact box
• The Baikal seal of Russia is the only freshwater seal in the world.
• Sea lion colonies sometimes have hundreds of thousands of sea lions in them.
• Monk seals are one of the few species to live in tropical water, such as the Caribbean Sea.

Find out more
Dolphin
Killer whale
Mammal
Whale

Shellfish

Shellfish are water creatures whose soft bodies are protected by hard shells. Like slugs, snails and octopuses, shellfish are molluscs. They are found in freshwater and saltwater all over the world.

△ When shellfish die, all that remains is the shell. If you go to the seaside, collect as many different shells as you can. Later, you can display them on a board with their names underneath them.

Fact box

• Some shellfish have just one shell, others have a pair.
• Shells are made from minerals. These make the shells very hard.
• Shellfish have existed on Earth for 600 million years.

◁ Most shellfish feed by filtering tiny food particles from the water. Some shellfish stay on the same rock all their lives. They anchor themselves with a single sucker foot, or by threads.

▽ Mussels have two matching shells that clamp shut when they are in danger. They hold on to rocks using threads that are so strong they can resist huge storm waves.

lambis shell **top shell**

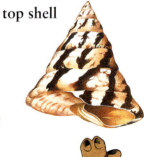

tiger cowrie

Find out more
Crab

Octopus and Squid

Shrimp and Prawn

Shrimps and prawns live in seas, rivers and lakes almost everywhere. They are related to lobsters but are smaller and are better swimmers. Prawns are slightly bigger than shrimps.

△ The pistol shrimp, which grows to about four centimetres long, has very large claws. It snaps them together to stun its prey.

▽ **1** Make an underwater viewer to look at shrimps and prawns in rock pools. Get an adult to cut the bottom off a clear plastic bottle. Stretch cling film over the cut end and secure with an elastic band.

▽ **2** You will need to keep still, as these animals are easily frightened.

◁ Shrimps and prawns often search for food on the seabed. They eat small plants and animals. They swim by flicking their fan-like tails.

Norway lobster

ghost shrimp

male common prawn

female common prawn

common shrimp

Find out more
Crab
Fish
Food
Shellfish

Tiger

Tigers are the biggest of all cats. They live in the grasslands and forests of Asia, where their striped coat gives them good camouflage when they hunt.

△ Female tigers give birth to between one and three cubs. The cubs stay with their mother for over a year.

△ A tiger slowly stalks its prey, a deer, through the long grass. When it is close enough, it makes a sudden dash, leaps onto the deer's back and knocks it down. A quick bite to the neck kills the deer.

◁ Tigers are hunted for their beautiful coats, and for their bones and body parts, which are used in traditional Chinese medicine. Because of this, tigers are nearly extinct.

Find out more
Cat (wild)
Cheetah
Leopard
Lion

Toucan

Toucans live in the tropical forests of the Americas. Their colourful beaks are thought to frighten off other birds. Although the beak is almost as big as the bird's body, it is very light. Toucans also have long tails to help them balance.

▽ Toucans gather in the treetops to roost and to feed on fruit. In order to swallow, they have to juggle their food in their beaks, then toss back their heads and catch it.

Fact box

- There are almost 40 species of toucan. The largest are up to 60cm long.
- The larger toucans sometimes eat eggs, small birds, frogs and lizards.
- Toucans are some of the noisiest birds in the forest. Their calls include loud croaks, barks and hoots.

▷ Bristles at the end of the toucan's long tongue act like a brush, helping it to hold on to its food.

◁ The hornbills of Africa, Asia and some Pacific islands also have large beaks. They get their name from the horny structure on top of their beaks, which are strong enough to crush small reptiles.

Find out more

Bird

Flamingo, Heron and Stork

Hummingbird

The publisher would like to thank the following for contributing to this book:

Photographs
Page 3, 4 Lyndon Parker; 6 Planet Earth Pictures; 7 Tony Stone Images; 9 Lyndon Parker; 12, 13, 14 Oxford Scientific Films; 15 Lyndon Parker; 16, 17, 21, 22 Andy Teare Photography; 23, 24 Oxford Scientific Films; 26, 27 Lyndon Parker; 30 Oxford Scientific Films; 31 Lyndon Parker *t*, Oxford Scientific Films *b*; 33 Oxford Scientific Films; 34 Lyndon Parker; 35 Lyndon Parker *t*, Oxford Scientific Films *m*; 36 Lyndon Parker; 37 Oxford Scientific Films; 38 Planet Earth Pictures; 39, 41 Lyndon Parker; 42, 44, 45 Oxford Scientific Films; 46 Andy Teare Photography; 47 Oxford Scientific Films; 49 Lyndon Parker; 52 Lyndon Parker *t*, *mr*, Oxford Scientific Films *ml*; 53 Andy Teare Photography *t*, Lyndon Parker *b*; 56, 58 Lyndon Parker; 59 Planet Earth Pictures *t*, Oxford Scientific Films *m*; 61 Lyndon Parker *tr*, Andy Teare Photography *tl*; 63 Lyndon Parker; 64 Tony Stone Images *ml*, Oxford Scientific Films *b*; 70, 71 Oxford Scientific Films; 72 Andy Teare Photography; 76 Oxford Scientific Films; 77 Lyndon Parker; 78, 80 Oxford Scientific Films; 81 Andy Teare Photography; 84 Oxford Scientific Films; 86 Andy Teare Photography *t*, Oxford Scientific Films *br*; 87 Andy Teare Photography; 88 Oxford Scientific Films; 89 Lyndon Parker; 90 Andy Teare Photography; 92 Lyndon Parker; 94, 96, 97 Oxford Scientific Films; 98 Lyndon Parker; 99 Planet Earth Pictures; 100 Oxford Scientific Films; 101, 104 Lyndon Parker; 106 Oxford Scientific Films; 107 Andy Teare Photography; 108, 109 Oxford Scientific Films; 111, 112, 113 Lyndon Parker; 114 Andy Teare Photography *t*, Oxford Scientific Films *m*; 116 Oxford Scientific Films; 118 Oxford Scientific Films *t*; Planet Earth Pictures *m*; 119 Andy Teare Photography; 120 Planet Earth Pictures; 121 Oxford Scientific Films *m*, Lyndon Parker *b*; 123 Planet Earth Pictures; 124 Andy Teare Photography; 125 Planet Earth Pictures; 126, 128 Oxford Scientific Films; 129 Lyndon Parker; 130, 131 Oxford Scientific Films

Artists
Graham Allen, Norman Arlott, Mike Atkinson, Craig Austin, Peter Barrett, Caroline Bernard, Robin Bouttell (Wildlife Art Agency), Peter Bull, John Butler, Robin Carter (Wildlife Art Agency), Jim Channel, Dan Cole (Wildlife Art Agency), David Cook, Richard Draper, Brin Edwards, Cecelia Fitzsimons (Wildlife Art Agency), Wayne Ford (Wildlife Art Agency), Chris Forsey, Ray Greenway, Nick Hall, Darren Harvey (Wildlife Art Agency), David Holmes, Steve Howes, Mark Iley (Wildlife Art Agency), Ian Jackson (Wildlife Art Agency), Martin Knowelden, Terence Lambert, Mick Loates, Bernard Long, Andrew Macdonald, Alan Male (Linden Artists Ltd), David Marshall, Doreen McGuinness, Brian Mcintyre, G. Melhuish, William Oliver, R.W. Orr, Nicki Palin, Bruce Pearson, Andie Peck (Wildlife Art Agency), Bryan Poole, Clive Pritchard (Wildlife Art Agency), John Rignall (Linden Artists Ltd), Steve Roberts (Wildlife Art Agency), Bernard Robinsons, Eric Robson (Garden Studio Illustrators' Agents), G. Robson, Mike L. Rowe (Wildlife Art Agency), Peter David Scott (Wildlife Art Agency), Guy Smith (Mainline Design), M. Stewart (Wildlife Art Agency), Mike Taylor (Garden Studio Illustrators' Agents), Joan Thompson, Treve Tamblin, Guy Troughton, Wendy Webb, Lynne Wells (Wildlife Art Agency), David Whatmore, Ann Winterbottom, David Wood (Wildlife Art Agency), David Wright, T. K. Wayte (David Lewis Management)

Models
Zak Broscombe Walker, Kechet Buckle Zetty, Martha Button, Jennifer Ching, Yazmina Faiz, Ellie French, Jonathan Hodgson, Christopher Jones, Peter Kemp, Ellie Kemp, Daniel MacArthur Seal, Jamie Nazareth, Jack Nazareth, Julia Nazareth, Iynn-ade Odedina, Okikade Odedina, Michael Rego, Rudi Russell, Leila Sowahan